101 Daily Math Challenges for Engaging Your Students

Hey There!

Welcome to the 101 Daily Math Challenges workbook.

You're probably here because you know that your kids can have fun learning math when the material is visual and engaging.

This book shares a huge collection of math challenge questions and puzzles that are fun to solve and are sure to get your kids thinking algebraically (often way before they ever step foot inside an algebra class!).

These challenges can be shared with kids, at all grade levels, in your math classroom, and at home.

Enjoy,
Anthony :)

TABLE OF CONTENTS

How can you use this workbook? …………………… 03

Looking to print? …………………… 05

Algebraic Challenges

Basic (1-10) …………………… 06

Intermediate (11-20) …………………… 17

Advanced (21-30) …………………… 28

Mult. & Division Focus (31-40) …………………… 39

Fractions Focus (41-50) …………………… 50

Decimals Focus (51-55) …………………… 61

Negative Numbers Focus (56-60) …………………… 67

Misc. Visual Math Puzzles (61-86) …………………… 73

Holiday Math Puzzles (87-101) …………………… 100

Answer Key & Hints …………………… 117

About the Author …………………… 124

About *Mashup Math* …………………… 125

References …………………… 126

A Few Ideas for Using These Challenges

- As warm-ups or exit activities at the beginning or end of class.

- As extra credit or homework assignments.

- As a component to lessons on topics including problem-solving, order or operations, fractions, decimals, area models, negative numbers, and more!

- As a supplement for differentiating pre-existing lessons to provide more opportunities for visual, collaborative, and/or hands-on learning

How to Print the Challenges

1.) Select the question that you want to print.

2.) Right-click on the page and select *PRINT*.

3.) Select the number of copies you want.

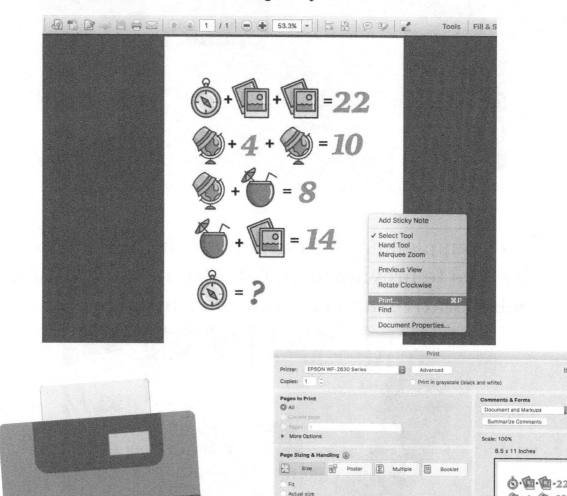

MASHUP MATH | Denver, CO | © 2017, get free stuff at www.*MashupMath.com*

Challenges 1-10
BASIC

Includes elements of…

✓ simple algebraic thinking

✓ variables and symbolic representation

✓ basic addition and subtraction

✓ substitution

✓ strategic problem solving

✓ logical thinking

✓ commutative property of addition

Name: _____ **Date:** _____

Challenge #1 of 101

🐼 + 🐼 + 🐼 = **21**

🐍 + 🐼 = 🦝

🐼 + 🐍 = **11**

🐼 + 🦝 + 🐍 = **?**

Name: _____   **Date:** _____

Challenge #2 of 101

$$\text{fish} + \text{beans} + \text{fish} = \text{skewer}$$

$$26 - \text{skewer} = \text{watermelon}$$

$$\text{watermelon} + \text{watermelon} = 2$$

$$\text{fish} + \text{fish} = \text{watermelon} + 9$$

$$\text{skewer} - \text{beans} = \;?$$

Challenge #3 of 101

🚀 − 9 = 🪐

🪐(saturn) = 🚀

7 + 1 = 🪐 + 🪐

🪐 + 🪐(saturn) + 🚀 = ?

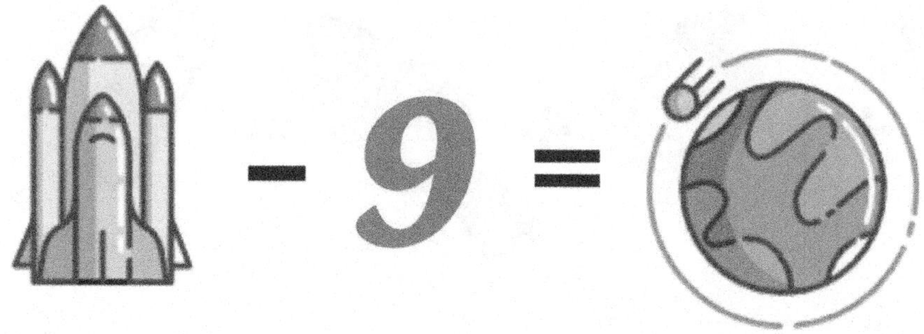

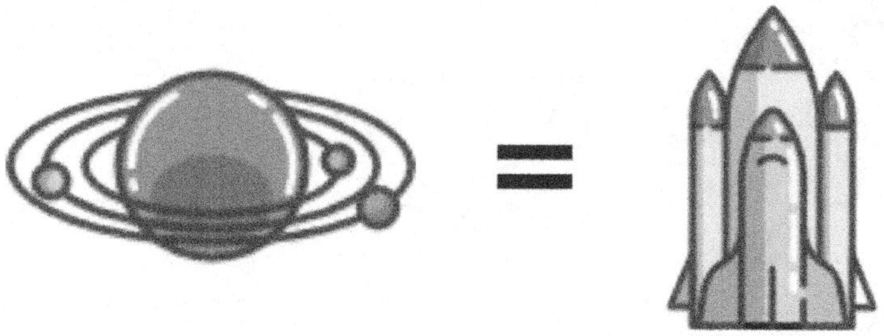

Name: _____   Date: _____

Challenge #4 of 101

🍕 = 🥣 + 🍔 + 🍅

🥣 + 🍔 = **7**

🥣 − 🍔 = **1**

9 + 🍕 = **18**

🍔 + 🍅 + 🍕 = **?**

Name: _____ Date: _____

Challenge #5 of 101

Name: _____ **Date:** _____

Challenge #6 of 101

$$20 = \text{🟡} + \text{🎮}$$

$$\text{🎮} + \text{🎮} + \text{🎮} = 36$$

$$\text{🟡} + \text{🟡} = \text{⚡}$$

$$\text{⚡} - \text{🎮} = \text{?}$$

Challenge #7 of 101

🏴‍☠️ + 🍾 + 🏴‍☠️ = **18**

☸️ + 💀 + ☸️ = **21**

🍾 = ☸️ − **3**

☸️ = 💀

🏴‍☠️ + 🍾 = **?**

Challenge #8 of 101

📍 + ❤️ = 15

⭐ + ⭐ = 26

⭐ − ❤️ = 3

📍 + ❤️ − ⭐ = ?

Name: _____   Date: _____

Challenge #9 of 101

🐻 − 🐞 = **1**

🐻 + 🐘 = **16**

11 = 🦊 + 🐞

🐘 = 🐻

🦊 + **3** + 🐻 = **?**

Challenge #10 of 101

$$2P + V = 60$$
$$2B + P = 30$$
$$B - M = 3$$
$$V = P$$
$$M + P + B = \,?$$

Answer: $2 + 20 + 5 = 27$

Challenges 11-20
INTERMEDIATE

Includes elements of...

✓ intermediate algebraic thinking

✓ variables and symbolic representation

✓ properties of zero

✓ substitution

✓ strategic problem solving

✓ logical thinking

✓ commutative property of addition

✓ associative property of addition

✓ order of operations

Challenge #11 of 101

$$7 - (2 + 1) = \text{🐻}$$

$$\text{🐧} + \text{🐧} = \text{🦭}$$

$$\text{🦭} - 3 = \text{🦭}$$

$$\text{🐻} + 10 = \text{🦭}$$

$$\text{🦭} + \text{🐧} - \text{🐻} = \text{?}$$

Challenge #12 of 101

🐦 + ▶ = 🎵

8 = 🐦 + 🐦

📷 + 📷 + 📷 = 🎵

▶ − 🐦 = 1

📷 + 🎵 − ▶ = ?

Challenge #13 of 101

$$\text{Duck} - \text{Car} = \text{Bear} + \text{Bear}$$

$$\text{Bear} + \text{Car} = 9$$

$$\text{Car} - \text{Bear} = 1$$

$$\text{Train} - \text{Bear} = \text{Duck}$$

$$\text{Duck} + \text{Train} = \ ?$$

Name: _____ **Date:** _____

Challenge #14 of 101

🧭 + 🖼️ + 🖼️ = 22

🌐 + 4 + 🌐 = 10

🌐 + 🥥 = 8

🥥 + 🖼️ = 14

🧭 = $?$

Name: _____ **Date:** _____

Challenge #15 of 101

🫐 + 🫐 + 🍒 = 27

🫐 = 🍒

14 − 🫐 = 🫐

🍒 + 🫐 − 🫐 = ?

Name: _____   **Date:** _____

Challenge #16 of 101

Lion + Hippo + Lion = 7

Rhino + Hedgehog + Rhino = 24

Rhino = Hedgehog

Hedgehog − Hippo = 3

Rhino + Lion + Rhino = ?

Name: _____ **Date:** _____

Challenge #17 of 101

Batman + Batman − Ninja = *17*

Batman(grey) + Koala + 3 = Batman(dark)

Koala + Batman(grey) = *7*

Batman(grey) + Ninja + Koala = *?*

Name: _____ **Date:** _____

Challenge #18 of 101

🍕 + 🍔🍟 + ☕ = 🍨

🍕 + ☕ = 13

🍨 − 🍔🍟 = 🍕 + ☕

🍔🍟 + 🍨 = 27

🍕 + 🍨 + ☕ = ?

Challenge #19 of 101

🥰 − 😠 + 😰 = 😐

😠 − 😰 = 😰

🥰 = 😠 + 😰 + 😰

2 + 😠 = 12

😐 − 11 = ?

Challenge #20 of 101

🚲 + ⛽ = 🚌 + 3

🚲 + 7 = 🚌

⛽ = 🚲

🚌 + ⛽ − 🚲 = ?

Challenges 21-30
ADVANCED

Includes elements of…

✓ advanced algebraic thinking

✓ variables and symbolic representation

✓ properties of zero

✓ substitution

✓ advanced multiplication and division

✓ logical thinking

✓ commutative property of addition and multiplication

✓ associative property of addition and multiplication

✓ advanced order of operations

Name: _____   Date: _____

Challenge #22 of 101

🇺🇸 + 🇧🇷 = 🇦🇺 + 1

🇺🇸 + 🇩🇰 + 🇩🇰 = 🇧🇷

🇦🇺 × 🇩🇰 = 0

🇦🇺 − 4 = 1

🇺🇸 × 🇧🇷 + 🇦🇺 = $?$

Challenge #23 of 101

$$\text{pencils} + \text{pencils} = \text{USB}$$

$$\text{pencils} - \text{pencils} = \text{USB} - 14$$

$$\text{USB} + \text{printer} = 15 + \text{laptop}$$

$$\text{laptop} = 1 \div \text{laptop}$$

$$\text{printer} = \;?$$

Challenge #24 of 101

$$\text{shirt} \times \text{lipstick} = \text{umbrella}$$

$$\text{shoe} - \text{umbrella} = 8$$

$$\text{lipstick} = \text{umbrella}$$

$$\text{shoe} \times \text{shoe} = 100$$

$$\text{shoe} - \text{shirt} \times \text{umbrella} = \,?$$

Challenge #25 of 101

🐘 + 🐘 = 🦩 + 🐍

🦒 ÷ 🐍 = 🦒

🐍 + 🦩 = **8**

🦩 − 🦒 = 🐍

🦒 × 🐘 = **?**

Challenge #26 of 101

🌙 + 🗽 = 🌙 + ⛩️

🌉 + ⛩️ = 🗽 + 5

🌙 + 🌉 − 4 = 8

🌉 × 🌙 = ?

Challenge #27 of 101

🏆 + 🎥 + 🌍 = 50

🏆 + 🏆 − 🏆 = 50 − 🌍

🎥 × 🌍 = 0

🌍 + 🌍 − 🌍 = 9

🏆 × 🎥 × 🌍 = ?

Challenge #28 of 101

$$\text{Play} \times 3 + \text{Drive} = G$$

$$42 \div G = \text{Drive} - 7$$

$$\text{Drive} - 1 = M + M$$

$$M = 4 \div 2 \times 2$$

$$G - \text{Play} \times M = \, ?$$

Name: _____ **Date:** _____

Challenge #29 of 101

🐢 ÷ 🐢 × 🦀 = 🐦

🦀 + 🐦 = **10**

🐢 − **1** + 🐦 = 🐟

🐟 = 🐢 + 🦀 − **1**

🐢 − **1** + 🦀 = **12**

🐢 + 🐦 × 🐟 = **?**

Challenge #30 of 101

🌱 + 📱 − 🌱 + 📱 = 🌱

🌲 = 💧 + 💧 + 💧

12 = 🌲 ÷ 3 + 🌲

🌲 − 💧 = 🌱

📱 × 🌱 × 💧 = ?

Challenges 31-40
FOCUS ON MULTIPLICATION & DIVISION

Includes elements of…

✓ variables and symbolic representation

✓ multiplying and dividing by zero and one

✓ substitution

✓ advanced multiplication and subtraction

✓ commutative property of multiplication

✓ associative property of multiplication

✓ advanced order of operations

✓ undefined values

Challenge #31 of 101

🧁 × 🍰 = 🍪 ÷ 🧁

🍪 × 2 = 8 × 8

🧁 = 🧁 ÷ 🍨

🍰 × 🍨 = 2

🍪 ÷ 🧁 × 🍰 = ?

Challenge #32 of 101

shoe × sweater × feather = 0

shoe × (sunglasses+mustache) = 15

(sunglasses+mustache) × feather = 12

shoe × feather = 20

shoe × sweater × (sunglasses+mustache) = ?

Challenge #33 of 101

🔵🔵🔵 ÷ 😺 = ⚡

$1 - ⚡ = ⚡$

😺 × ⚡ = 🔵🔵🔵

$42 ÷ 🔵🔵🔵 = 6$

⚡ + ⚡ = 1

😺 ÷ 🔵🔵🔵 × ⚡ = ?

Answer: 1

(Pokéballs = 7, Snorlax = 14, Pikachu = 0.5)

Challenge #34 of 101

🐨 × 🐨 × 🐨 = 27

🐨 × 🐵 = 🦙 × 🦝

🦝 × 🦙 = 18

🦙 − 🦝 = 🦝

🐵 × 🦙 × 🦝 = ?

120

Challenge #36 of 101

🏠 = 🌳 × 🌳 × 🌳

🥛 × 9 × 🥛 = 729

🥛 × 🌳 × 🥛 = 162

🌳 × 🏠 × 🥛 = ?

🏠 × 🌳 × 🥛 = ?

🥛 × 🏠 × 🌳 = ?

Challenge #37 of 101

🌟 ÷ 🧨 = 1

🌵 × 🌟 × 🌵 = 64

👢 = 🧨 × 🌟

🌟 = 🌵

🧨 × 👢 × 🌟 = ?

Challenge #38 of 101

$$\text{avocado} \times \text{avocado} \times \text{avocado} = 64$$

$$\text{cheese} \times \text{pepper} = 100$$

$$\text{pepper} \div \text{cheese} = \text{avocado}$$

$$\text{cheese} \times \text{pepper} \div \text{avocado} = \text{?}$$

Name: _____ Date: _____

Challenge #39 of 101

🧭 ÷ 🚢 = *0*

🌴 × 🧭 × 🚢 = 🧳

🌴 ÷ 🚢 = 🚢

🚢 ÷ *4* = 🧭 + *1*

🧳 + 🌴 × 🚢 = **?**

MASHUP MATH | Denver, CO | © 2017, get free stuff at www.MashupMath.com

Challenge #40 of 101

soccer ÷ paddle = paddle

paddle ÷ flag = undefined

bowling × paddle = 36

paddle ÷ bowling = 4

flag ÷ soccer + paddle × bowling = ?

Challenges 41-50
FOCUS ON FRACTIONS

Includes elements of…

✓ variables and symbolic representation

✓ dividing by zero and one

✓ substitution

✓ reducing fractions

✓ identifying equivalent fractions

✓ adding and subtracting fractions

✓ multiplying and dividing fractions

Name: _____   **Date:** _____

Challenge #41 of 101

🧟 + 🧟 + 🧟 = 🎃

1 = 🍲 + 🍲

🍲 = 🐱 + 🐱

🎃 − 🍲 = $\dfrac{1}{2}$

🧟 = ?   🐱 = ?

🍲 = ?   🎃 = ?

Challenge #42 of 101

$$1 = \dfrac{1}{\text{🦇}} + \dfrac{\text{🥷}}{\text{😀}}$$

$$\text{😀} - \text{🥷} = 1$$

$$\text{🦇} = \text{😀}$$

$$\text{😀} \times \text{🦇} = 25$$

$$\text{😀} + \text{🦇} - \text{🥷} = \,?$$

Name: _____ **Date:** _____

Challenge #43 of 101

🐒 + 🦒 + 🐰 = 4

1 = 🦩 ÷ 🦩

🦒 = 6 × 🐒

2 × 🐒 = 🦩

🦒 − 🐰 − 🐒 = ?

MASHUP MATH | Denver, CO | © 2017, get free stuff at www.MashupMath.com

Challenge #44 of 101

$$\dfrac{\text{🐭}}{\text{⚪}} + \dfrac{2}{\text{⚪}} + \dfrac{\text{🥚}}{4} = 2$$

$$1 - \dfrac{\text{🐭}}{\text{⚪}} = \text{🧑}$$

$$\text{🧑} + \text{🧑} = \dfrac{1}{2}$$

$$\text{🥚} = \text{🐭}$$

$$\text{⚪} \times \text{🥚} \times \text{🧑} = \;?$$

Challenge #45 of 101

$$\frac{1}{\text{🍩}_A} \times \frac{1}{\text{🍩}_A} \times \frac{1}{\text{🍩}_A} = \frac{\text{🍩}_B}{27}$$

$$\text{🍩}_C + \text{🍩}_C = \frac{2}{3}$$

$$\text{🍩}_D = 3 \times \text{🍩}_C$$

$$\text{🍩}_D = \text{🍩}_C \times \text{🍩}_A$$

$$\text{🍩}_A \times 8 \times \text{🍩}_C = \text{?}$$

$$\frac{\text{🐻}}{100} = \frac{\text{🦍}}{\text{🐯}}$$

$$\frac{4}{\text{🐯}} = \frac{1}{\text{🦍}}$$

$$25 \times \frac{1}{5} = \text{🦍}$$

 −  −  = ?

Challenge #47 of 101

$$\frac{7}{\text{banana}} - \frac{\text{milk}}{\text{banana}} = \frac{\text{chocolate}}{3}$$

$$\text{chocolate} = \text{milk} + \text{milk}$$

$$\text{chocolate} \div 4 = \frac{1}{2}$$

$$\frac{7}{\text{banana}} + \frac{2}{\text{banana}} + \text{chocolate} = \ ?$$

Challenge #48 of 101

$$48 \times \frac{\text{microscope}}{\text{bulb}} = \text{cookie}$$

$$\frac{\text{microscope}}{\text{bulb}} + \frac{\text{microscope}}{\text{bulb}} = \frac{\text{cookie}}{24}$$

$$\text{cookie} \times \frac{1}{2} = 6$$

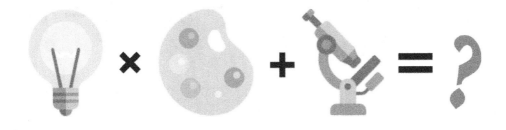

Challenge #49 of 101

$$\frac{18}{\text{monitor}} + \frac{\text{heart}}{3} + \frac{\text{virus}}{\text{virus}} = \text{pill}$$

$$\text{heart} = \text{virus}$$

$$\frac{1}{10} + \frac{\text{monitor}}{\text{pill}} = 1$$

$$\text{monitor} + \text{heart} + \text{pill} - \text{virus} = \ ?$$

Challenge #50 of 101

👧 − 💎 = $\dfrac{5}{7}$

$\dfrac{💎}{\text{chest}} = 0$

$2 = 👧 + \text{chest}$

$\text{chest} = \dfrac{9}{7} + 💎$

$\text{chest} - 👧 = \,?$

Challenges 51-55
FOCUS ON DECIMALS

Includes elements of…

✓ **variables and symbolic representation**

✓ **substitution**

✓ **algebraic thinking and problem-solving**

✓ **order of operations**

✓ **adding and subtracting decimals**

✓ **multiplying and dividing decimals**

Name: _____   **Date:** _____

Challenge #51 of 101

🏅 + ✈️ + 🎆 = 1.35

1 − 🏅 = 0.5

0.15 = 🎆 − ✈️

🎆 = 🏅

✈️ + 2 + 🎆 = ?

Challenge #52 of 101

$$\text{(blue robot)} + \text{(blue robot)} + \text{(rover)} = \text{(face)}$$

$$\text{(dark robot)} = \text{(face)}$$

$$\text{(rover)} + 1.4 = 3$$

$$1 = 0.8 + \text{(blue robot)}$$

$$\text{(dark robot)} - \text{(rover)} - \text{(blue robot)} = \,?$$

Challenge #53 of 101

$$3J = 0.75 + L$$
$$L + T = 2J$$
$$1 = T + T$$
$$W + L = T + T$$
$$L \times W = 0$$
$$J + T + W = \,?$$

Answer: 1.75

Challenge #54 of 101

$8 - \text{tent} - 1 = \text{fire}$

$\text{knife} = \text{fire} - 1.1$

$6.2 = \text{tent} + 1 + \text{tent}$

$\text{tent} + \text{knife} + \text{fire} = ?$

Challenge #55 of 101

🍇 + 0.97 + 🥝 = 2

🍉 ÷ 🥝 = 5

4 = 🍉 − 🥝

.09 = 🍇 + 🍇 + 🍇

🍉 − 🍇 × 4 = ?

Challenges 56-60
FOCUS ON NEGATIVES

Includes elements of...

✓ advanced algebraic thinking

✓ variables and symbolic representation

✓ properties of negative numbers

✓ substitution

✓ adding and subtracting negative numbers

✓ multiplying and dividing negative numbers

✓ commutative property of addition and multiplication

✓ associative property of addition and multiplication

✓ order of operations

Challenge #56 of 101

$9 + 🦜 = 🐑$

$🦆 = 🦘 \times -3$

$🦘 + 🦜 = 🦆 \times -1$

$3 = 🦘 + 10$

$? = 🦘 \times 🐑 + 🦆$

Challenge #57 of 101

🤿 + 🌴 = 🩳

1 + 🩳 + 2 = 0

🥤 = − 🤿

4 = 🤿 + 🩳

🌴 − 🩳 = 🥤

🤿 × 🌴 + 🥤 = ?

Challenge #58 of 101

$$\text{surfer} \times \text{couple} \times \text{girl} = \text{horse}$$

$$1 \div \text{couple} = -1$$

$$\text{horse} = \text{girl} \times -(\text{surfer})$$

$$\text{girl} + \text{couple} = 5$$

$$\text{couple} \times 30 = \text{horse}$$

$$\text{horse} + \text{surfer} \times \text{couple} = \text{?}$$

Name: _____   Date: _____

Challenge #59 of 101

🧁 ÷ 🍦 = 2

🍭 = 🧁 × 2

-8 = 🍪 + 🍦

0 = 🍪 - 🍦

🍦 = -27 ÷ 3

🍭 × 2 + 🍦 × 3 = ?

Challenge #60 of 101

 ×  +  =

 = 7 − 3 × 3

 +  = −11

 ×  = 28

 × 2 =

 ×  × +  = ?

Challenges 61-86
VISUAL PUZZLES

Includes elements of…

✓ number sense and number webs

✓ value tables

✓ algebraic functions with inputs and outputs

✓ order of operations

✓ geometric representations of values

✓ visual mathematics

✓ pattern recognition

✓ writing functions

✓ algebraic modeling

✓ area models and hundreds charts

✓ working with models, diagrams, and arrays

Name: _____ Date: _____

Challenge #61 of 101

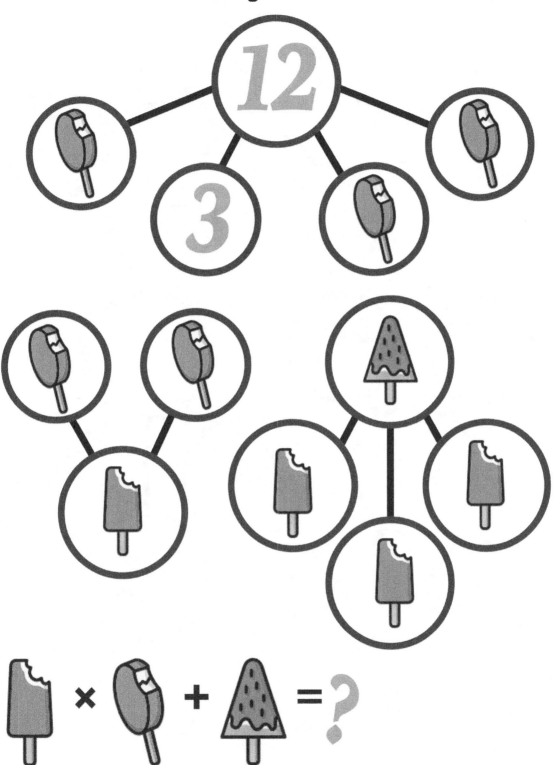

Challenge #62 of 101

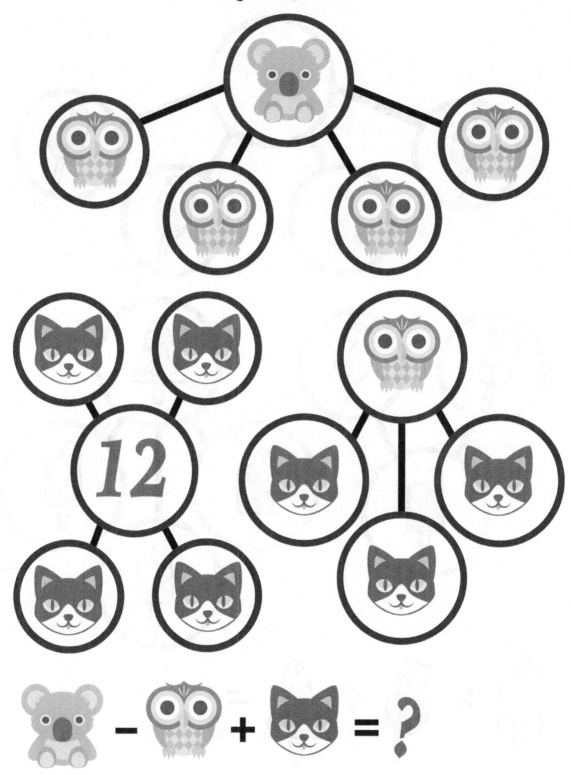

Name: _____ **Date:** _____

Challenge #63 of 101

input	output
1	4
2	
3	6
4	7
5	8

input	output
3	7
7	15
9	
11	23

input	output
	9
4	7
8	5
12	
16	1

input	output
5	24
4	
3	16
2	12
1	8

Can you find the value of each of the following?

Challenge #64 of 101

input	output
0	🍍
5	5
🕶️	10
15	15
20	20

input	output
8	18
4	🕶️
7	16
9	👣
🍍	2

input	output
24	👣
20	🍄
16	🕶️
14	🎮
12	🍍

input	output
🍍	🍍
🎮	🕶️
🕶️	👣
🍄	30
👣	💎

Can you find the value of each of the following?

Challenge #65 of 101

$(36 - 4) \div 4 =$ 🏔️

$24 +$ 🏔️ $\times 3 =$ 🗺️

🗺️ $\div ($ 🏔️ $\times 2) =$ 🧭

$4 ($ 🗺️ $\div$ 🏔️ $+$ 🧭 $) =$ 🥾

🏔️ $\times$ 🧭 $- 4 - 5 \times$ 🧭 $=$ 🎒

🥾 $-$ 🎒 $- ($ 🏔️ $\div 2) \times$ 🧭 $=$ 🌰

Name: _____ Date: _____

Challenge #66 of 101

Each of the boxes below represents 100.

Assign a value for each symbol using using the choices below. You can use a value more than once.

5 49 27 6 17 34 65 30

Challenge #67 of 101

Name: _____   **Date:** _____

Challenge #68 of 101

Challenge #69 of 101

Challenge #70 of 101

Challenge #71 of 101

Name: _____   Date: _____

Challenge #72 of 101

case #1

case #2

case #3

 Does there appear to be a pattern or relationship?

 Sketch what case #4 and #5 would look like?

 How many cinnamon rolls would be in case #10?

 What about case #100?

Name: _____   Date: _____

Challenge #73 of 101

 Can you find the missing value in each sequence?

Challenge #74 of 101

 How many lollipops will be in case #6 and #9?
What about case #100?

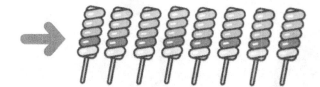

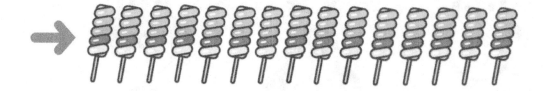

Challenge #75 of 101

Can you find the missing value in each case?

Column 1: 3, 5, 8, 12, ?
Column 2: 3, 6, 12, 24, ?
Column 3: 3, 10, 31, 94, ?

Name: _____   Date: _____

Challenge #76 of 101

 Find the value of each icon in the multiplication table below:

Challenge #77 of 101

 Find the value of each icon in the multiplication table below:

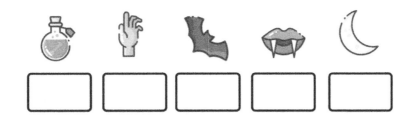

Challenge #78 of 101

 Find the value of each icon in the multiplication table below:

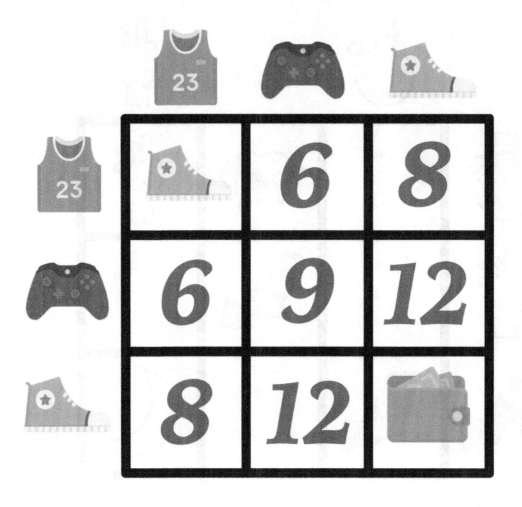

Challenge #79 of 101

Find the value of each icon in the multiplication table below:

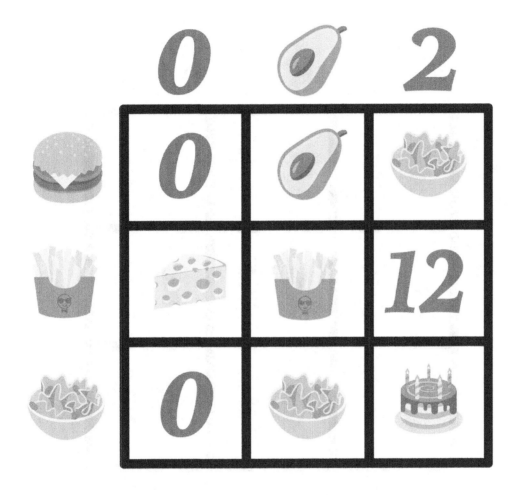

Challenge #80 of 101

Find the value of each icon in the multiplication table below:

Challenge #81 of 101

In the triangle below, the sum of the three values on each side is 9. Using each of the values beneath the triangle only once, assign a number to each circle to complete the triangle.

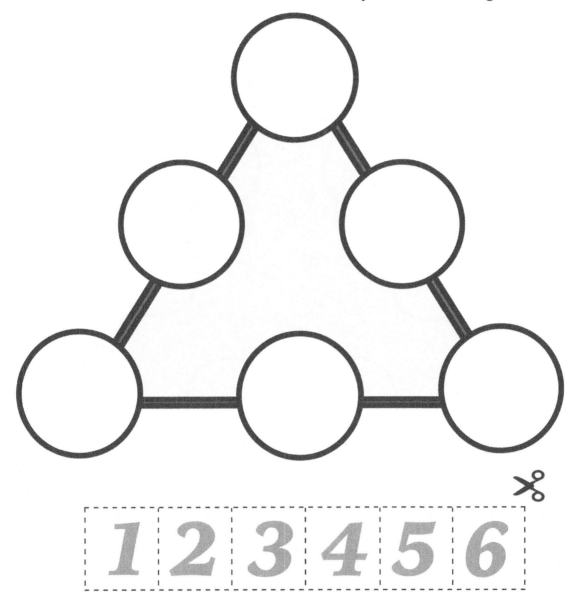

Challenge #82 of 101

In the triangle below, the sum of the four values on each side is 17. Using each of the values beneath the triangle only once, assign a number to each circle to complete the triangle.

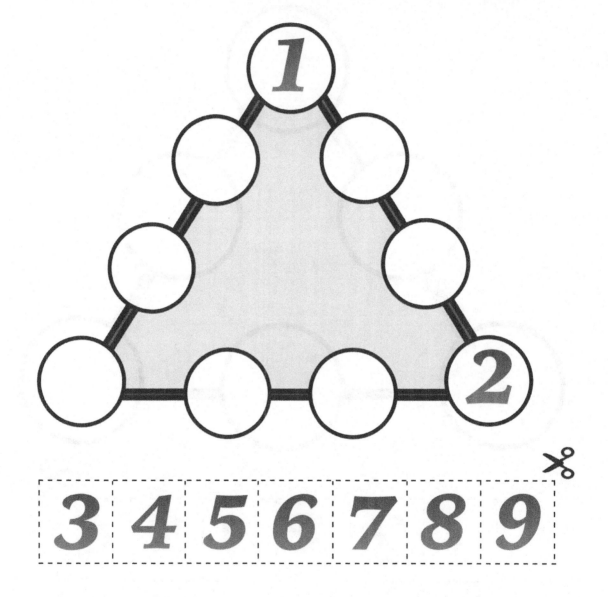

Challenge #83 of 101

If the multiplication table below represents the value 91, find the value of each icon.

Challenge #84 of 101

 If the multiplication table below represents the value 714, find the value of each icon.

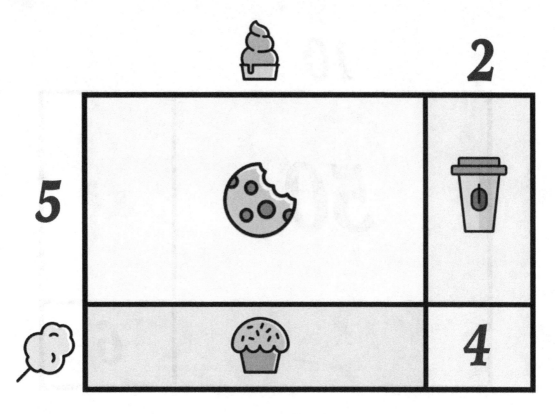

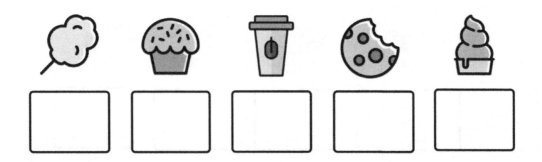

Name: _____ **Date:** _____

Challenge #85 of 101

 Find a value for each icon in the area model below so that it represents the value 7,200.

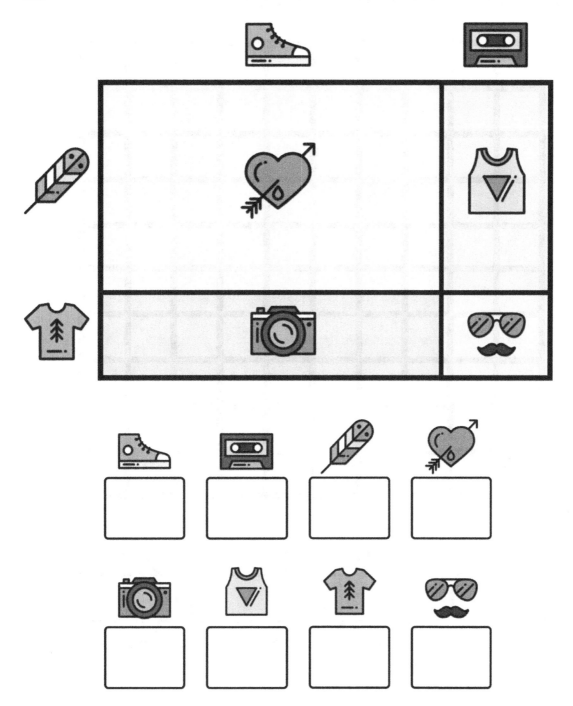

Name: _____   **Date:** _____

Challenge #86 of 101

 If the diagram below represents 250, find the value of each color.

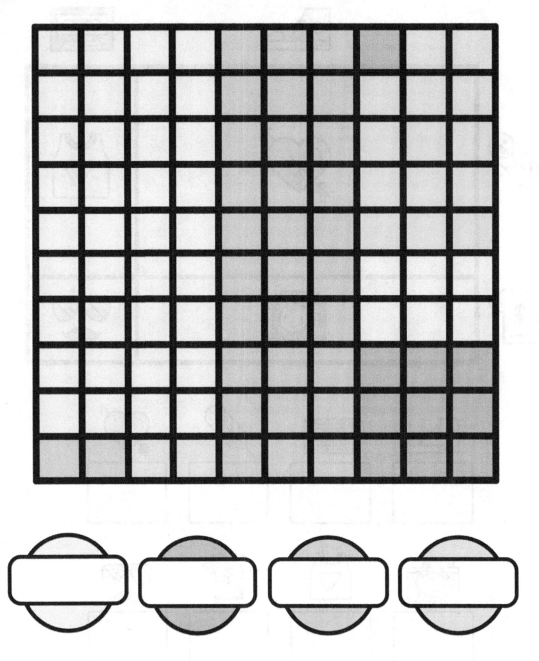

Challenges 87-101
CELEBRATE HOLIDAYS

Includes elements of...

✓ advanced algebraic thinking

✓ variables and symbolic representation

✓ properties of zero

✓ substitution

✓ strategic problem solving

✓ logical thinking

✓ commutative property of addition

✓ associative property of addition

✓ order of operations

Name: _____ **Date:** _____

Challenge #87 of 101

Happy New Year!

🪩 = 🎆 − 2

🎆 + 9 + 🎆 = 27

🪩 = 🎈 − 9

🍾 + 🍾 = 🎈

🎈 × 🪩 − 🎆 × 🍾 = ?

Challenge #88 of 101

Happy Groundhog Day!

🐹 + 🐹 − 🎩 = 🎈

10 = 110 ÷ 🎈

🎈 − ☀️ = 7

🐹 − 3 = ☀️

🎈 × 🎩 − 🐹 × ☀️ = ?

Name: ______________________________ **Date:** __________

Challenge #89 of 101

Happy Valentine's Day!

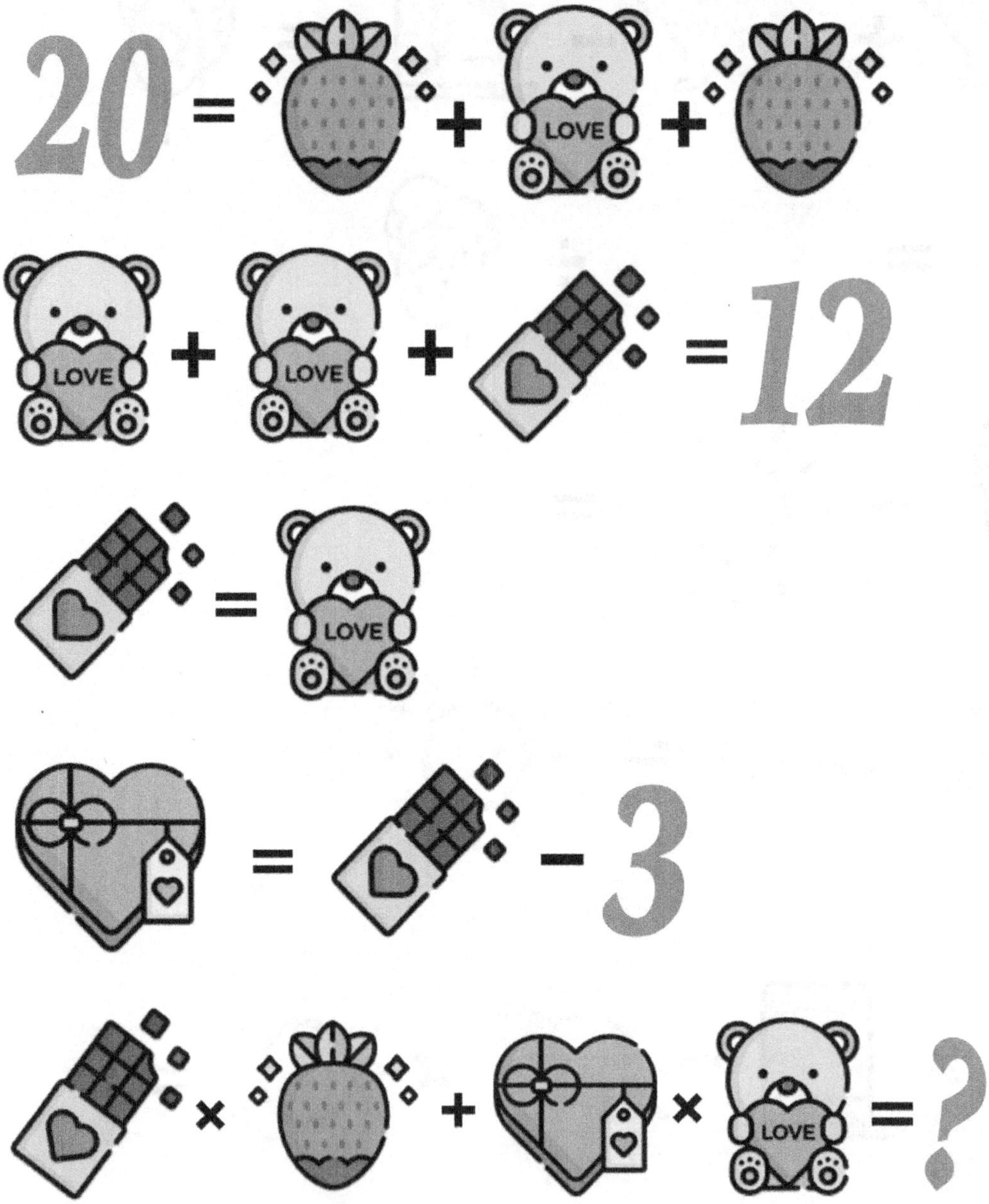

Happy Chinese New Year!

🐉 = 🌳 + 🌳 + 🌳

🌳 = 5 × 🧺

24 ÷ 3 = ☯ + 3

🧺 = ☯

🐉 − 🧺 × ☯ = ?

Happy St. Patrick's Day!

Challenge #91 of 101

🏳️ + 🐻 + 🐻 = 9

🍯 − 3 + 🍯 = 13

14 = 🍯 + 🎩

🐻 + 4 = 🎩

🏳️ × 🐻 + 🍯 × 🎩 = ?

Name: _____ Date: _____

Challenge #92 of 101

Happy April Fool's Day!

🙊 + ❓ = ☂️ × 🙂

☂️ × 3 = 🙂

14 − 🙂 = 14

7 = 4 + ❓ + 3

🙊 = ☂️

🙂 × ❓ × ☂️ × 🙊 = ❓

Happy Easter!

Challenge #93 of 101

🐰 + 🌸 + 🐰 = 9

🫘 = 🥚

🥚 × 🫘 × 🥚 = 8

🐰 = 🥚 − 🐰

🥚 × 🌸 − 🐰 + 🫘 = ?

Challenge #94 of 101

Happy Earth Day!

🌍 − 🌼 + 🚐 = 19

🕊 + 🚐 + 🕊 = 33

26 = 🌍 + 🚐

🚐 ÷ 🕊 = 1

🕊 × 🌼 − 🌍 = ?

Happy Arbor Day!

🌳 + 🌲 = 🌴 + 3

🌴 = 7 + 🌳

🌳 = 🌲

? = 🌳 + 🌲 + 1 − 🌴

May The Fourth Be With You!

Kylo × BB-8 ÷ Vader = Boba

Boba = Leia + Leia + Vader

BB-8 + Kylo = 15

Kylo − BB-8 = 7

19 × Vader = 38

Vader × Boba + Kylo × Vader = ?

Challenge #97 of 101

Happy Cinco de Mayo!

🥣 + 🥣 − 🇲🇽 = 15

🥣 − 🎩 = 3

🪇 = 4 × 4 ÷ 2

15 = 🎩 + 🪇

3 × 🇲🇽 − 🥣 = ?

Happy Halloween!

🎃 × 🧟 × 🐈 = 🧪

🧪 = 💀 + 💀 + 💀

🐈 × 7 = 7

🎃 ÷ 💀 = 🐈

8 − 🎃 = 🎃

🧪 + 🐈 = ?

Name: _____   Date: _____

Challenge #99 of 101

Happy Veterans Day!

🪖 = 🇺🇸 + 🇺🇸

🦅 = 8 − 🦅

🎖 = 🇺🇸 + 2

🇺🇸 = 🦅

🪖 + 🦅 − 🎖 = ?

Challenge #100 of 101
Happy Thanksgiving!

🍰☕ + 🦃 = 🥧 + 🏈

🥧 + 🍁 = 10

🦃 + 🦃 = 🍁 + 3

🍁 ÷ 🥧 = 1

17 = 🍰☕ + 🏈

🏈 × 🍁 + 🍰☕ = ?

Season's Greetings!

Challenge #101 of 101

🧦 × 🎄wreath × ☕ = 24

❄️globe = 🎄wreath

☃️ = 🌐 + 🌐 + 🌐

🎄 + 1 + 🎄 = 7

11 = ☃️ + ☕

☕ × ☃️ − 🧦 × 🌐 = ?

Are your students engaged?

Share your experience with fellow teachers + parents on Twitter and be sure to tag us!

@mashupmath

Answer Key

1.) Panda=7 Snake=4 Raccoon=11 ?=22 Hint: Follow the Panda	**2.)** Gummy Fish=5 Jelly Beans=15 Lollipop=25 Gummy Melon=1 ?=10 Hint: Start with the green gummies	**3.)** Rocket=13 Earth=4 Saturn=13 ?=30 Hint: Start on your home planet	**4.)** Pizza=9 Chips & Dip=4 Hamburger=3 Tomato=2 ?=14 Hint: Which two numbers have a sum of 7 and a difference of 1?
5.) Monkey=10 Rabbit=2 Fox=7 Ostrich=5 ?=5 Hint: Follow the bunny	**6.)** Pac-Man=8 Gameboy=12 Thunder Bolt=16 ?=4 Hint: You need a Gameboy before you can play Pac-Man	**7.)** Pirate=7 Bottle=4 Wheel=7 Skull=7 ?=11 Hint: The wheel and skull are interchangeable	**8.)** GPS Icon=5 Heart=10 Star=13 ?=2 Hint: The north star leads the way
9.) Bear=8 Lady Bug=7 Elephant=8 Fox=4 ?=15 Hint: The bear and the elephant are interchangeable	**10.)** Pikachu=20 Jigglypuff=20 Zubat=5 Bulbasaur=2 ?=27 Hint: Pikachu and Jigglypuff represent the same value!	**11.)** Polar Bear=4 Penguin=7 Lion=14 Walrus=11 ?=14 Hint: Follow the polar bear.	**12.)** Twitter=4 YouTube=5 Spotify=9 Instagram=3 ?=7 Hint: Tweet first!
13.) Rubber Ducky=13 Race Car=5 Teddy Bear=4 Train=17 ?=30 Hint: What two numbers have a sum of 9 and a difference of 1?	**14.)** Compass=4 Photos=9 Globe=3 Coconut=5 ?=4 Hint: Start with the globe!	**15.)** Raspberry=7 Blueberries=13 Cherries=7 ?=1 Hint: 14 subtracted by what number is equal to that same number.	**16.)** Lion=1 Hippo=5 Rhino=8 Porcupine=8 Hint: The rhino and the porcupine are interchangeable.

MASHUP MATH | Denver, CO | © 2017, get free stuff at www.MashupMath.com

17.) Batman=10 Cyclops=3 Hulk + Flash =7 ?=10 Hint: You won't be able to find the individual values of Hulk and Flash, but knowing that their sum is 7 is enough.	18.) Pizza + Tea=13 Burger & Fries=7 Ice Cream=20 ?=33 Hint: What two values have a sum of 27 and a difference of 13?	19.) Love Eyes=20 Angry Red=10 Sick Green=5 Eye Roll=15 ?=4 Hint: Deal with your anger before you do anything.	20.) Bike=10 Gas Pump=10 Bus=17 ?=17 Hint: You can replace any bus with the sum of a bike and seven.
21.) Kangaroo=3 Alligator=3 Panda=1 Hippo=5 ?=9 Hint: The kangaroo and the alligator must equal the same value.	22.) USA=3 Brazil=3 Australia=5 Sweden=0 ?=14 Hint: The sum of any number and zero is that same number.	23.) Pens=7 USB=14 Printer=2 Laptop=1 Hint: The value of the pens is a single-digit odd number.	24.) Shirt=10 Lipstick=2 Umbrella=2 Sneaker=10 Hint: 100 is a perfect square.
25.) Elephant=4 Flamingo=7 Snake=1 Giraffe=6 ?=24 Hint: Any number divided by one is that same number.	26.) Egypt=7 England=5 Liberty=China ?=35 Hint: While you can't be sure of the values of Liberty and China, you know that they must be equal.	27.) Trophy=41 Camera=0 Earth=9 Hint: Find the value of Earth first.	28.) YouTube=4 Chrome Symbol=9 Google=21 Mail=4 ?=5 Hint: Order of operations is the key!
29.) Turtle=8 Crab=5 Seagull=5 Fish=12 ?=68 Hint: The crab and the seagull must be equal.	30.) Seedling=6 Phone=3 Tree=9 Water Drop=3 ?=54 Hint: Find the value of the tree first.	31.) Cupcake=4 Chocolate Cake=2 Cookie=32 Ice Cream=1 Hint: Any value divided by one equals itself.	32.) Sneaker=5 Sweater=0 Feather=4 Glasses=3 ?=0 Hint: The product of any value and zero is always zero.

MASHUP MATH | Denver, CO | © 2017, get free stuff at www.MashupMath.com

33.) Pokeballs=7 Snorlax=14 PokeCoin=1/2 ?=1 Hint: A PokeCoin is one-half of a PokeDollar!	34.) Koala Bear=9 Monkey=2 Lamb=6 Raccoon=3 ?=36 Hint: Multiplication is commutative.	35.) Pancake=10 Strawberry=20 Egg=2 Coffee=80 ?=120 Hint: How many tens do you need to make 200?	36.) Corn=2 Barn=8 Milk=9 All ?'s=144 Hint: Multiplication is commutative.
37.) Star=4 Dynamite=4 Cactus=4 Boot=16 ?=256 Hint: The star and the cactus are interchangeable.	38.) Avocado=4 Cheese=5 Pepper=20 ?=25 Hint: Think about possible values whose product is 100.	39.) Compass=0 Ship=4 Palm Tree=16 Suitcase=0 ?=64 Hint: You can only have zero in the numerator of a fraction.	40.) Soccer=144 Ping Pong=12 Golf=0 Bowling=3 ?=36 Hint: The quotient of any value and zero is undefined.
41.) Zombie Hand=1/3 Pumpkin=1 Caldron=1/2 Cat=1/4 Hint: Start with the caldron!	42.) Batman=5 Cyclops=4 Deadpool=5 ?=6 Hint: Batman and Deadpool are the same value.	43.) Monkey=1/2 Giraffe=3 Bunny=1/2 Flamingo=1 ?=2 Hint: Do you know how to multiply a whole number by a fraction?	44.) Rat=3 PokeBall=4 Egg=3 Trainer=1/4 ?=3 Hint: Look for a common denominator when adding fractions.
45.) Chocolate Frosting=3 Pink Frosting=1 Red Velvet=1/3 ?=8 Hint: Do you know how to multiply fractions?	46.) Bear=25 Gorilla=5 Tiger=20 ?=0 Hint: Fractions are equivalent when they are equal after being simplified.	47.) Bananas=9 Milk=1 Chocolate=2 ?=3 Hint: Do you know how to check if two or more fractions are equivalent?	48.) Microscope=1 Light Bulb=4 Paints=12 ?=49 Hint: When you multiply a value by one-half, you cut it in half.

49.) EKG Monitor=9 Hear=21 Virus=21 Pill=10 ?=19 Hint: Any non-zero value divided by itself equals one!	**50.)** Rich Lady=5/7 Jewels=0 Treasure Chest=9/7 ?=4/7 Hint: In a fraction, zero can only be in the numerator!	**51.)** Ribbon=0.5 Paper Airplane=0.35 Bottle Rocket=0.5 ?=2.85 Hint: The ribbon and the bottle rocket are the same value.	**52.)** Orange Robot=0.2 Pink Robot=1.6 Green Robot=2 Dark Blue Robot=2 ?=0.2 Hint: Start with the pink robot!
53.) Jellyfish=0.25 Lobster=0 Whale=0.5 Turtle=0.5 ?=1.25 Hint: Let the turtle lead the way!	**54.)** Tent=2.6 Camp Fire=4.4 Swiss Army Knife=3.3 ?=10.3 Hint: Start your trip by setting up your tent!	**55.)** Grapes=0.03 Kiwi=1 Watermelon=5 ?=4.88 Hint: Eat the grapes first!	**56.)** Parrot=-14 Sheep=-5 Duck=21 Kangaroo=-7 ?=56 Hint: Start with the Kangaroo and then hop around.
57.) Goggles=7 Palm Tree=-10 Swim Trunks=-3 Iced Tea=-7 ?=-77 Hint: Find the value if the swim trunks first (they're negative!)	**58.)** Surfer=5 Wrestlers=-1 Dancer=6 Horseback Rider=-30 ?=-35 Hint: The quotient of any positive value and any negative value is always negative.	**59.)** Muffin=-18 Ice Cream=-9 Cotton Candy=-36 Cookie=1 ?=-99 Hint: Find the value of the ice cream first.	**60.)** Sneaker=-4 Water Bottle=-7 Gym Bag=-26 Headphones=-2 ?=30 Hint: Find your headphones before you hit the gym!
61.) Chocolate Covered=3 Grape=6 Strawberry=18 ?=36 Hint: When dividing 12 into 4 equal parts, what is the value of each part?	**62.)** Cat=3 Owl=9 Koala=36 ?=30 Hint: Start with the cats!	**63.)** Ratatat=5 Snorlax=11 Catepillar=19 Pikachu=0 Zubat=3 Jigglypuff=20 Hint: Look for patterns!	**64.)** Pineapple=0 Sunglasses=10 Footprints=20 Mushroom=15 Gem=40 Hint: The value of the footprints is 20

65.) Mountain=8, Map=48, Compass=3, Hiker=36, Backpack=5, Acorn=19 Hint: Follow order of operations!	66.) Star=49, Heart=27, Smiley Face=17, Thunder Bolt=34, Balloon=49, Moon=65, Coffee=30, Cherry=6, Play Button=5	67.) Orange Juice=36, Grocery Bag=18, Fruit=9, Coffee Cup=3, Chef's Hat=2 Hint: Think about values that are divisible by both 3 and 4 and have a sum of 54.	68.) Ring Pop=15, Sour Melon=5, Strawberry Candy=10, Lollipop=3, Jelly Beans=2 Hint: Start from the top.
69.) Pirate=12, Bottle=6, Skull=3, Treasure=4, Hook=1 Hint: The value of the Pirate is 12.	70.) Ninja Turtle=42, Stormtrooper=14, Minion=7, Surgeon=20, Ironman=10 Hint: The value of the surgeon is 20.	71.) Pink Bar=16, Chocolate Bar=8, Purple Bar=2, Ice Cream Cup=24, Ice Cream Cone=3 Hint: The value of the pink bar is two-thirds the value of the ice cream cup.	72.) Case 4=25 cinnabuns, Case 5=36 cinnabuns Case 10=121 cinnabuns Case 100=10,201 $(n+1)^2$ where n is the case number
73.) Purple=25 (increasing by consecutive odd numbers) Green=81 (each value is the 3 times the difference of the previous two values) Pink=15 (each value is the sum of the difference of the two previous values and the previous value)	74.) Case 6=35 lollipops, Case 9=80 lollipops Case 100=9,999 lollipops $n^2 - 1$ where n is the case number	75.) ?=17 (increasing by consecutive integers) ?=48 (each value is twice the previous) ?=283 (increasing by three times the difference of the previous two numbers)	76.) Boy w/ Orange Shirt=0, Boy w/ Blue Sleeves=1, Boy w/ Flat Top=2, Girl w/ Flower=4, Girl w/ Yellow Shirt=5, Boy w/ Orange Hair=0
77.) Potion=1, Green Hand=3, Bat=6, Vampire Lips=2, Moon=18	78.) Jersey=2, Controller=3, Sneaker=4, Wallet=16	79.) Cheese=0, Burger=1, Fries=6, Salad=2, Avocado=1, Birthday Cake=4	80.) Pikachu=-4, Charmander=5, Jigglypuff=5, Snorlax=2, Dratini=8, Ratatat=-8, Meouth=25, Caterpillar=-20

81.)

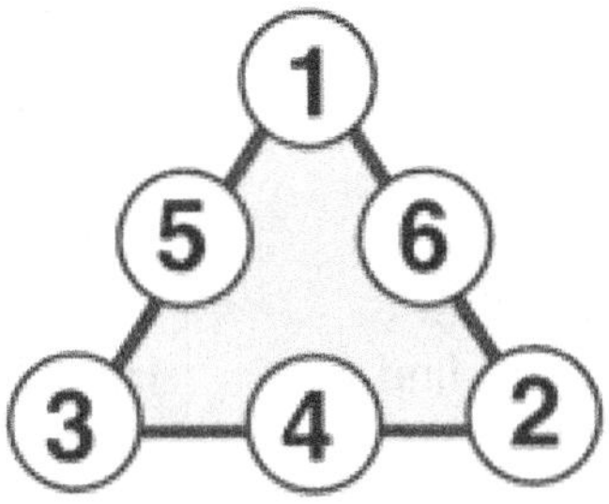

82.) Here are two possible solutions, but there are more!

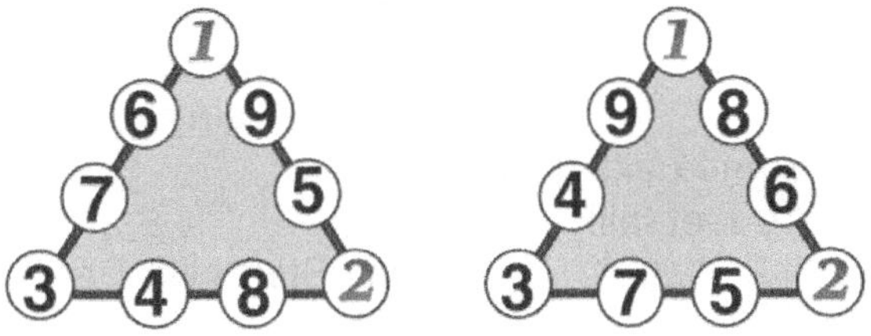

83.)
Banana=3
Strawberry=5
Grape=15
Pineapple=20
Orange=2

84.)
Cookie=500
Ice Cream=100
Cotton Candy=2
Muffin=200
Coffee=10

85.)
Sneaker=100
Cassette=20
Feather=50
Shirt=10
Heart=5000
Camera=1000
Jersey=1000
Glasses=200

Hint: $120 \times 60 = 7{,}200$

86.)
Each box equals 2.5

Green=105
Blue=80
Pink=25
Orange=40

Holidays

87.) New Years
Fireworks=9
Disco Ball=7
Balloons=16
Champagne=8
?=40

Hint: Start with the fireworks!

88.) Groundhog Day
Groundhog=7
Top Hat=3
Balloons=11
Sun=4
?=5

Hint: Start with the balloons!

89.) Valentine's Day
Strawberry=8
Teddy Bear=4
Chocolate Bar=4
Box of Chocolates=1
?=36

Hint: The teddy bear and the chocolate are equal the same value!

90.) Chinese New Year
Dragon=75
Bonsai Tree=25
Gift Basket=5
Yin-Yang=5

Hint: Start with the Yin-Yang!

91.) St. Patrick's Day
Flag=5
Teddy Bear=2
Pot of Gold=8
Green Hat=6
?=58

Hint: Start with the pot of gold!

92.) April Fool's
Monkey=0
Smiley=0
Umbrella=0
Question Mark=0
?=0

Hint: The answer to this challenge doesn't amount to anything!

93.) Easter
Bunny=1
Flower=7
Egg=2
Jelly Beans=2
?=15

Hint: Begin with the bunny!

94.) Earth Day
Earth=15
Flower=7
Van=11
Dove=11
?=62

Hint: Any non-zero value divided by itself is equal to one.

95.) Arbor Day Oak Tree=10 Pine Tree=10 Palm Tree=17 ?=4 Hint: Some oaks grow to be 10 feet tall!	96.) May the Fourth Kylo Ren=11 BB-8=4 Darth Vader=2 Boba Fett=22 Princes Leia=10 ?=66 Hint: Start with Darth Vader!	97.) Cinco de Mayo Chips and Dip=10 Flag=5 Sombrero=7 Maracas=8 ?=5 Hint: Use the maracas to find everything!	98.) Halloween Pumpkin=4 Zombie Hand=3 Cat=1 Skull Candle=3 Potion=12 ?=13 Hint: The pumpkin is the key!
99.) Veteran's Day Soldiers=8 Flag=4 Eagle=4 Star=6 ?=6 Hint: Start with the eagle!	100.) Thanksgiving Cake=9 Turkey=4 Pie=5 Football=8 Leaves=5 ?=49 Hint: The leaves and the pie have equal values.	101.) Season's Greetings Stocking=4 Wreath=3 Hot Cocoa=2 Snowman=9 Snow Globe=3 ?=6 Hint: Find the wreath first!	

About the Author

Anthony Persico is a math teacher and education enthusiast just like you! He is the chief content creator and founder of *MashUp Math*. Anthony has taught thousands of students in NY, VA, and CO as well as across the globe via 20,000+ subscribers on his YouTube channel. He joins Jo Boaler as an advisor to Amazon Education's *With Math I Can* campaign and is a featured blogger for *Harvard Education Journal.* He loves to hike, travel, cook, and play with his dog, Zoey.

Made in the USA
Monee, IL
23 November 2024